anythink

P9-DEH-211

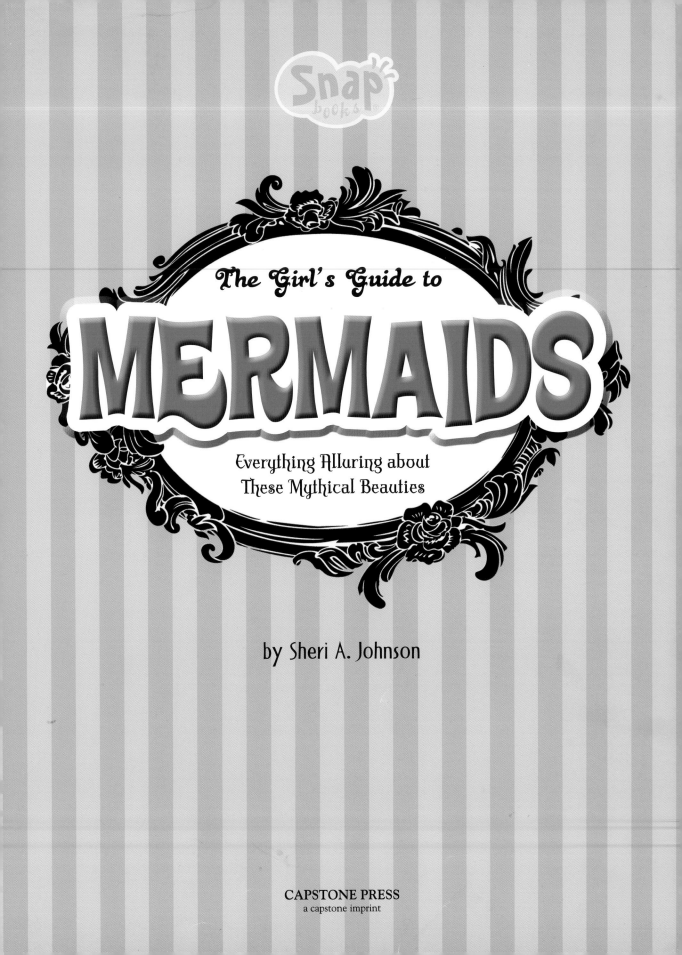

Snap books

The Girl's Guide to

MERMAIDS

Everything Alluring about
These Mythical Beauties

by Sheri A. Johnson

CAPSTONE PRESS
a capstone imprint

Snap Books are published by Capstone Press,
151 Good Counsel Drive, P.O. Box 669, Mankato, Minnesota 56002.
www.capstonepub.com

Books published by Capstone Press are manufactured with paper
containing at least 10 percent post-consumer waste.

Library of Congress Cataloging-in-Publication Data
Johnson, Sheri.
 The girl's guide to mermaids : everything alluring about these mythical beauties / by Sheri A. Johnson.
   p. cm. — (Snap books. Girls' guides to everything unexplained)
 Includes bibliographical references and index.
 Summary: "Describes the mystery, cool characteristics, and allure of mermaids, including historical and
contemporary examples"—Provided by publisher.
 ISBN 978-1-4296-6557-5 (library binding)
 1. Mermaids—Juvenile literature. I. Title. II. Series.

 GR910.J64 2012
 398.21—dc22   2011010026

Editorial Credits
Editor: Mari Bolte
Designer: Tracy Davies
Media Researcher: Svetlana Zhurkin
Production Specialist: Laura Manthe

Photo Credits:
Alamy: Paz Spinelli, 4, Photos 12, 29 (top); The Bridgeman Art Library: Private Collection/Look and Learn, 11
(bottom); Cover of *Teenage Mermaid* by Ellen Schreiber, Katherine Tegen Books, 25 (right); Cover of *The Last
Olympian* by Rick Riordan, Disney Hyperion Books for Children, 25 (left); Cover of *The Tail of Emily Windsnap* by
Liz Kessler, Candlewick, 25 (middle); Dreamstime: Martina Orlich, 13 (top), Trishastreasuresorg, 14; DVD cover
of *Aquamarine*, 20th Century Fox, 27 (right); Getty Images: Mark Kolbe, 11 (top); iStockphoto: Theresa Tibbetts,
cover (mermaid silhouette); Mary Evans Picture Library, 12, 20, Arthur Rackham, 18, 19, Illustrated London
News, 8; Newscom: akg-images, 17, Album/20th Century Fox/Vince Valitutti, 29 (bottom), Album/Nippon Televison
Network Corporation/Studio Ghibli, 27 (left), 29 (middle), Album/Warner Bros., 26 (left), 28 (top), SHNS file photo
courtesy Nintendo, 28 (bottom), SHNS photo courtesy HarperCollins Children's Books, 26 (right); Shutterstock:
Athanasia Nomikou, cover (swimming mermaids), KathyGold, 6, Kerry L. Werry, 16, LampLighterSDV, cover
(bubbles), Sergey Popov, cover (light), Tiberiu Stan, 13 (bottom), timy, cover and throughout (water drops), Titus
Manea, 21, Vilena, 5; Svetlana Zhurkin, 9, 15

Printed in the United States of America in North Mankato, Minnesota.
032011
006110CGF11

Contents

Mermaids have been swimming in people's imaginations for thousands of years. These tailed sea-dwellers have been sighted around the globe. Mermaids were once considered bad luck, appearing before storms and other disasters. Thanks to modern movie star mermaids like Ariel and Aquamarine, they now enjoy a better **reputation**.

reputation : one's character, as judged by other people

These creatures of the sea have many secrets. Although people have believed in mermaids for centuries, nobody has ever proven their existence. People all over the world are attracted to the mysterious mermaids.

So are mermaids friendly fish folk or threatening tailed terrors?

The earliest mermaid story dates back to around 1000 BC in an Assyrian legend. A goddess loved a human man but killed him accidentally. She fled to the water in shame. She tried to change into a fish, but the water would not let her hide her true nature. She lived the rest of her days as half-woman, half-fish.

Later the ancient Greeks whispered tales of fishy women called sirens. These beautiful but deadly beings lured sailors to their graves. Many sailors feared or respected mermaids because of their association with doom.

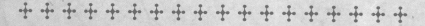

Are you seeing a fish, a woman, or a mermaid?

Around the world, other mermaid stories are told. Drowning sailors have been rescued by women who live among the waves. Mermaids love handsome men. They like to find young sailors and nurse them back to health under the sea. Their magic prevents the sailors from drowning. But be careful—once a mermaid claims you, it's very difficult to escape.

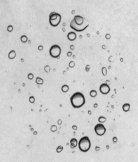

But where do mermaids come from?

An Irish legend tells that mermaids are women who are being punished. An old European folktale says that mermaids are the drowned children of an unknown **pharaoh**. The ancient Greeks made them a part of their **mythology**. But which tale is right?

pharaoh : another name for an Egyptian king

mythology: old or ancient stories that connect people with their past

Some people believe that mermaid sightings can be explained by science.

They think that people who see mermaids are actually seeing regular animals, such as manatees or giant squid. In 1492 Italian explorer Christopher Columbus saw strange beasts off the coast of Haiti. He did not find these plump gray creatures attractive. Even after seeing their whiskers, he assumed they were mermaids.

Scientists don't believe in mermaids because a mermaid's body has never been recovered. But stories and eyewitness reports of these creatures have appeared all over the world. In 1608 men aboard explorer Henry Hudson's ship reported seeing a mermaid off the east coast of Greenland. Hudson recorded that the mermaid had black hair, a porpoise tail, and speckled skin like a fish.

In 2009 a town in Israel offered a $1 million reward to anyone who could photograph a mermaid on local beaches. Locals insist that they have seen a little girl with a fish tail who only appears at sunset. But nobody has yet proven the existence of the mermaid.

Flip through these pages to learn more about the most famous **myth** of the sea. Then think it over and decide for yourself. Do mermaids really exist or are they just the stuff of legend?

myth: a story told by people in ancient times

Chapter Two

Fin-tastic Features

What do mermaids look like? You'd think it would be easy to tell, right? Just look for a woman with a fish tail instead of legs. But not all mermaids are alike! Here are some fantastic features that will help you decide whether or not you've just seen a mermaid.

Tails: When we imagine mermaids, most of us picture a sleek, scaly fish tail. But some mermaids have tails that are split in half. Others have legs under their fish tails so they can walk on land. And there are some mermaids that don't have fish tails at all. Mermaids with the tails of dolphins, eels, or snakes have been spotted. Some even claim they have seen reverse mermaids. These women have legs on the bottom and the bodies of fish!

A professional diver named Hannah Fraser is the closest thing to a real mermaid. Hannah is a professional mermaid. She wears a silicone tail when she swims in the ocean. Using the power of her lungs and tail, Hannah can dive up to 91 feet (28 meters) on a single breath of air.

Hannah Fraser

Physical features: Mermaids are meant to blend in with the ocean. Their skin is usually green or blue, although very pale mermaids have been seen. Blond mermaids are common, but mermaids with black, green, or blue hair are out there too.

Male merfolk are called mermen. They are usually less attractive than mermaids. Many mermen grow beards and carry tridents. In *The Last Olympian*, Percy Jackson sees merpeople with blue skin, glowing green eyes, and shark teeth. His half-brother, Triton, is a merman. His green skin and double tail set him apart from Percy.

Where they live: Mermaids live in both freshwater and in the sea. They have the rare ability of breathing both underwater and on land. The Zora people in The Legend of Zelda games live anywhere underwater. They can sometimes live on land, but only for short periods of time.

Families: Mermaids give birth to live babies, rather than laying eggs like a fish. They usually raise their families underwater. But those who fall in love with mortal men may choose to live on land. In the past, people thought they could spot a landbound mermaid by her babies. Offspring of a mermaid would have webbed fingers or toes.

A mermaid and her water baby

Voices: Some mermaids are able to speak above water. Others, such as the merpeople in *Harry Potter and the Goblet of Fire*, have their own language that can only be understood well underwater. The sirens of ancient Greece had beautiful singing voices. The sound of their voices would tempt sailors to abandon their missions or put men to sleep.

Accessories: In terms of style, mermaids don't have much to work with. After all, how many ways can you dress up a fish tail? But there are two things they're rarely seen without—a mirror and a comb. They are often pictured sunbathing on rocks, admiring their reflections while brushing their long, beautiful hair.

FACT

Some sharks, rays, and skates lay egg sacs that scientists call "mermaid's purses."

SWEET OR SCARY?

When it comes to meals, mermaids love fish. But don't let this fool you—some mermaids have vampire-like tastes and crave flesh and blood. Others have frightening, pointed teeth designed to catch and eat other sea creatures.

Even with a mouthful of sharklike teeth, mortal men find mermaids very beautiful. There are many legends of men drowning while trying to capture a mermaid. Others simply tell stories of men who wish to live among the merpeople. One Greek myth tells the story of a fisherman who wants to live in the sea. He refuses to return to land, and the gods turn him into a merman.

The mystery of mermaids is a story humans love to tell. Something about these mythical creatures draws us in. What we know about mermaids comes from legends and stories that have been told for many years.

FACT

Some mermaids are vain. They like being sought out by humans. Others are shy creatures that only come to the surface during a full moon.

Chapter Three
Fish Tales

Scary-sounding stories about mermaids are told all around the world. Greek merpeople known as lamias have eel tails and hiss when they talk. Children and the blood of men are their favorite foods.

In Germany, freshwater nixies lure people to drowning by playing enchanting music. Scottish and Irish selkies are half human and half seal. They can shed their seal skin and walk on land. If selkies are unable to find their skin, they will be trapped in their human form. Across Africa, a mermaid named Mami Wata is a powerful healer who keeps a snake as a pet. She has great power and can use her magic for good or evil.

No matter the country of **origin**, mermaid stories usually reveal unhappy, rather than cruel, creatures. Many myths tell of a sea maiden who falls in love with a mortal man. The stories usually don't have a happy ending.

FACT

The word lamia means "large shark" in Greek.

origin: the source of something

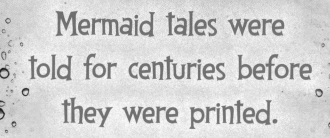

Mermaid tales were told for centuries before they were printed.

The German tale *Undine* was one of the first mermaid tales ever printed. The story follows the life of a sea spirit raised by a fisherman and his wife. Undine meets a knight and the two marry.

Undine

Undine tells her new husband that she is the daughter of a water prince. If her husband were to ever leave, she would have to return to the sea. He promises to stay with her. But one day in anger, he curses her and sends her back into the water. In revenge, she kills him with a kiss. After the funeral, she turns into a water fountain.

Mermaid tales have been told around the world.

Another famous tale is the story of Melusine.
This mermaid made her husband promise to leave her
completely alone for a full day and night every month.
One night he snuck to her room and peeked through
the keyhole. He saw his wife bathing with her fish
tail sticking out from the side of the tub! Melusine
heard his startled cry and lept into the river below.
She disappeared from his life forever.

Melusine (center)

Even the Little Mermaid doesn't originally end with a happily ever after.

In the traditional story by Hans Christian Anderson, the mermaid will die if she can't win the prince's heart. But the prince doesn't fall in love with the mermaid. In fact, he marries someone else!

The sea witch tells the mermaid that she can save her own life by killing the prince. She will also have to return to the sea. Instead of killing the prince, the mermaid throws herself off a cliff and is turned into an air spirit.

statue of the Little Mermaid in Copenhagen, Denmark

QUIZ: What Kind of Mermaid are You?

Do you dream of swimming out to sea? Take this quiz to find out what kind of fish-finned mermaid you would be!

1. What is your favorite color?

a. blue-green

b. hot pink

c. anything metallic

d. black

2. What is your ideal hairdo?

a. green and wavy

b. long and blond

c. dark and mysterious

d. black and choppy

3. What is your favorite sea creature?

a. I only like other merpeople.

b. Oysters—that's where pearls come from, after all!

c. No creatures recognized by science!

d. I love sharks—the scarier, the better!

4. What do you wear in the ocean?

a. My fin and beautiful hair.

b. Anything that will look good both above and below water!

c. A seaweed cape.

d. A bracelet made from sea urchins.

5. Do you have supernatural skills?

a. My ability to shed my tail for legs.

b. Catching cute boys with my great vocals.

c. My magic is my ability to make myself beautiful.

d. Isn't being a mermaid supernatural enough?

Look through your answers to discover what kind of mermaid you are. If you have:

Mostly As: You're a mermaid through and through. Who cares what they do on the surface? You can walk on land, but who would want to?

Mostly Bs: You're a traditional romantic. You love your life at sea but yearn to meet your very own Prince Charming.

Mostly Cs: You're like a modern-day sea witch. Forget tentacles and bad hair. You take ocean magic to the next level and look good doing it!

Mostly Ds: You're spunky and punky. You take the ocean one wave at a time and don't let the little things get you down. You live your life at the edge of the ocean!

Chapter Four

Mermaids in the Media

Read, Watch and Learn

You may catch a glimpse of these alluring beauties on the silver screen or in the pages of your favorite book. Whether they're flitting through the seas of Narnia or flirting with Jack Sparrow in *Pirates of the Caribbean: On Stranger Tides*, audiences can't get enough of these fish-finned females!

READ IT: *The Last Olympian* by Rick Riordan

In the final book of the Percy Jackson and the Olympians series, Percy visits his father, Poseidon, god of the sea. The Greek gods are preparing for war against Kronos and his army of monsters. Merpeople play a big role in helping Poseidon protect the sea.

C READ IT: *The Tail of Emily Windsnap* by Liz Kessler

Emily Windsnap has never learned how to swim. She finally decides to take the plunge. But during her first lesson, her legs turn into a tail! She discovers that there is a whole mermaid society beneath the sea. Emily begins a search to find her mermaid father and learn the truth about her family's history.

C READ IT: *Teenage Mermaid* by Ellen Schreiber

Teenage Mermaid is a modern twist on the traditional mermaid story. A beautiful mystery girl rescues the main character, Spencer, from the sea. The only clue about the girl's identity is a silver locket she leaves behind. Flip through the pages of this book to find out if Spencer discovers his rescuer's identity!

WATCH IT: *Harry Potter and the Goblet of Fire* (movie)

The Triwizard Tournament sends Harry underwater. There he must face grindylows and a tribe of fierce merpeople. Watch to find out whether Harry gets there in time to save Ron and Hermione, or if his tale ends at the bottom of Black Lake.

READ IT: *The Lion, the Witch, and the Wardrobe* by C. S. Lewis

Mermaids make an appearance at the end of this classic fantasy. The land of Narnia is filled with many other mythical creatures, such as fauns, witches, and magical animals. Read more about merpeople and the adventures of the Pevensie children in the later book, *The Voyage of the Dawn Treader*.

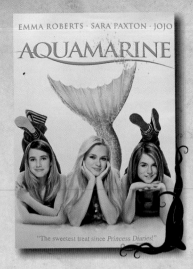

⚓ WATCH IT: *Ponyo* (movie)

A modern-day mermaid story, Ponyo is a goldfish kept in her father's underwater castle. Ponyo escapes but is washed onto a beach. A young boy named Sosuke rescues Ponyo, who turns into a human girl. The two children become friends. Watch the movie and find out if this magical girl remains human or returns to the sea.

⚓ WATCH IT: *Aquamarine* (movie)

One night, 12-year-olds Hailey and Claire find a mermaid in a swimming pool. The mysterious mermaid is Aquamarine. She has turned her tail into legs to search for true love. Can this spirited mermaid win the love of the handsome lifeguard, or will she be forced to return to sea alone?

MERMAID YEARBOOK

The Scariest Award:
Merpeople in *Harry Potter and The Goblet of Fire*

The unfriendly merfolk who confront Harry Potter during the Triwizard Tournament are not the sweet and soulful type.

Almost a Merman:
Link

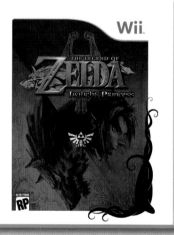

In the *Legend of Zelda: Twilight Princess*, the hero, Link, rescues the Zora prince. In return, he is rewarded with armor that allows him to breathe underwater.

Undersea Warriors:
Merpeople in
The Last Olympian

Poseidon's army needs merpeople to beat Hades and his monsters. Without the people of the sea, Poseidon would have lost control of the ocean forever.

Cutest Fish:
Ponyo

With the help of her friend Sosuke, Ponyo changes from a cute little goldfish into a cute little girl.

Modern~Day Mermaid:
Aquamarine

This young mermaid befriends two human girls. She also falls for a man before returning to the sea.

GLOSSARY

mortal (MOR-tuhl)—someone or something that will die

myth (MITH)—a story with a purpose; myths often describe quests or explain natural events

mythology (mi-THOL-uh-jee)—old or ancient stories told again and again that help connect people with their past

origin (OR-uh-jin)—the cause or source of something

pharaoh (FAIR-oh)—another name for an Egyptian king

reputation (rep-yuh-TAY-shuhn)—one's character, as judged by other people

silicone (SIL-uh-kohn)—a man-made material used to make lubricants, adhesives, and synthetic rubber

READ MORE

Rau, Dana Meachen. *Mermaids.* Bookworms Chapter Books: For Real? New York: Marshall Cavendish Benchmark, 2011.

Redmond, Shirley Raye. *Mermaids.* Monsters. Detroit: KidHaven Press, 2008.

Taylor, C. J. *Spirits, Fairies, and Merpeople: Native Stories of Other Worlds.* Plattsburgh, N.Y.: Tundra Books, 2009.

INTERNET SITES

FactHound offers a safe, fun way to find Internet sites related to this book. All of the sites on FactHound have been researched by our staff.

Here's all you do:

Visit *www.facthound.com*

Type in this code: 9781429665575

Super-cool stuff! Check out projects, games and lots more at
www.capstonekids.com

INDEX